Light-eater

Light-eater

by

Claire Marsden

First published 2025 by The Hedgehog Poetry Press,

5 Coppack House, Churchill Avenue, Clevedon. BS21 6QW

www.hedgehogpress.co.uk

ISBN: 978-1-916830-27-1

Cover Image © Mathew Harrison

Contents

I

Salt

I sit in the cafe, childless, and smile at the new mums with their babes.
They surround me like clouds.
I drink my coffee and wonder, which little dollop of joy, sweet as sea-glass, will grow up
to self-harm by the time the earth has sailed 11 times around the sun?
Which one, will have a mind so addled with distress that they'll live like a wild-eyed Alice, dark and bemused, stuck, behind the looking glass?

A baby giggles, and I taste salt in my mouth.

I had a baby, once, with a soul so fair, that if the birds had caught a glimpse, they would surely have fallen from the sky in praise.
We glowed with love, and peace, and tired enchantment. All milky-mouthed and soft-smiled.
Thoughts as tender as thistledown.
But you never know what dark waters will enter your home. Which cracks will let them in. You think you'll be educated enough to contain them. Loving enough, to hold them back.
The right nursery, the right school, the right friends. The museums and the art galleries. Organic food and bedtime routines. The laughter and the love. The love. Oh, the love.
I held you, once upon a time.

If those parents are lucky, they'll learn how to catch the escaping light, no matter how small, and bottle it, tight.
A drop to rest in. A starry crown of life.
They'll dream that you'll grow out of the lie that you aren't safe in this world or well enough to survive.
They'll sing spells to re-clothe you. Hymns to your heart. You are enough, my beloved.
You've been enough from the start.

Salt; in the untethering and crumbling we are tethered to you.

Funeral for a Womb

Womb: (n) wretched occasionally makes babies

ashes to ashes / dirt to dirt
good dirt / holy dirt
feed the dirt

a graveyard for all the women betrayed
by their bodies
some kind of homecoming

Spring

I took myself out for a walk,
and was greeted by the sea
announcing itself
upon the shore.
I tipped my hat, in recognition
of its beauty and strength,
the possibility of peace
stretching wide across its arms.
It bowed
in acknowledgement
of the power seeded deep within me.
Perhaps,
I shall wake it.

And God said...

Daughter,
I no longer dream of Eden.
Just a place
where you feel at home
in your own skin.

summer

the darkness was such
i hadn't even noticed
the lilies had bloomed

Mountain

"You are so strong,
like a mountain".
My dear,
Do not wish for blisters
and bleeding.
My strength was hard-won,
And even mountains crumble.

Light-eater

I sit
on the bed watching
thoughts fall.
Naproxen
     Codeine
  Paracetamol
You took them all, washed down with champagne.
A quiet Christmas cocktail.
Then returned to bed and slept.

The snow kept falling.

I go outside and open my mouth
to the sky.
To call. To catch.
To eat light.

Thoughts fall, it's okay.
I can swallow them
whole.

afternoon peace

shafts of light kiss trees
your hand touches the shadows
we rest in silence

Sight

The scales fell from my eyes,
And as I looked in mirror,
I saw myself standing tall,
defiantly,
as a winter daffodil on pillowed snow,
as a wildflower growing
between the cracks of old bricks.
As a joyous, tender, new-born kiss;
wondrous, and worthy, and whole.
Even the mind,
ungloved and wild,
whispered,
Amen.

Falling Stars

The wood was buried
under night
when uninvited you came
and sat
on the edge of my bed.
Watching.
Waiting.

Pale breath rising.

Look at me, you cried.
Look!
I closed my eyes.
Turned away my face.
You smiled, and crept closer. Breathed black
in my ear. Sat on my chest, and with sharpened teeth -
grinned.

I answered you,
with ink
and rage.
With falling stars
I pinned you
to that quaking page.
Then ate you for breakfast
with eggs
and coffee
and sunshine.
My words like daggers
in your blackened, bloodied mouth.
Such a feast.
And still, I eat.

The Susurrations of Trees

One day, while driving your car,
you will glance at your hands
and become startled
at how much they resemble your mother's.
Soft lines and delicate wrinkles
at home on your skin will stare back.
Through the open window, you'll hear trees
loosening their leaves.
They'll
fall
like
confetti
welcoming you.
Listen. Time leans in.

Life

You brought me to my knees,
reminded me of my fallibility.
My weaknesses
and wounds.
For that,
I thank you.
And offer you my smile.

II

The Visit

The unhurried weight of your embrace,
familiar,
at first touch.
Your tongue, gentled
with sunshine,
circles upon circles.
And our curiosity
swept clean.
Cleared.
Like the skies above.
Holy, empty, and filled
with knowing.
An unholy homecoming?
Perhaps.
Yet, even the angels smile.

The Gentle Dance

On 'After the Bath, Woman Drying her Neck', 1898 by Degas
(The painter and Painted)

I lay on my bed, naked,
after the bath,
Towels and fatigue
draped around me.
From my window I can see
ash trees swaying in the breeze.
But I am quietly told,
they are, in-fact,
dancing.
A gentle dance.
A deep-from-time dance.
My eyes fill with life.
Our bodies turn.
And like the dissolving drops
of glacial ice,
Fatigue retreats.

His

He described me like one of
Knight's paintings;
Distinctive
Forceful
Sensuous.
I think he should like to hang me
on the wall,
admire and study me,
not a single brushstroke overlooked.
His.
But I would never give him
such power,
my scars belong to another.

Death and Tulips

(I)

It was March when you died cold and grey the ground beneath my
shattered palms grasped at the living breath
breathe breathe
grasping to breathe I walk without you scratching the earth fingers
searching for tulip bulbs
they will flower soon

(II)

I woke up at 5am, wrote of death and tulips, then went back to sleep at
5.15am. You woke not long after, eyes wide and hungry. I held you in my
mouth, gently.
Your smile put death to shame.

The Edge of Yourself

You cocoon yourself in your routines -
Keep going. Stay steady.
An indwelling of the familiar. Your brain about to burst
through the cracks in your skull.
Easy now. Breathe.
At times you feel as though you are standing at the edge
of a volcano, staring
into its depths.
Too preoccupied, or tired, to look behind you.
To see me, sitting here, shining.
Patiently waiting. With love as bright as a thousand suns.
Trying so hard,
to turn away.

At first...

You don't know they will slice you open,
like a fish.
Scales laid bare to the sun.
They have voices that lull you to dream, mouths so warm,
they belie the teeth that cut—
(wounds as stunning as the arctic-blue eyes that can pull
the silk from your hips)
But when the cold wraps its legs around you,
you'll remember;
you were asleep on melting ice.

frozen ground

miles of frozen ground
even the solitary
crave warmth of friendship

The Dream

Where are your words that once fell like leaves? There is nothing
but bare earth at my feet.
I'll stand. I'll pause. Until the stars themselves are dead.
Lichen will grow in the hollows of my bones so ancient
it will start to speak.
How do I reconcile your absence from the groves? Your heat from my
hand?
Birds still call where we lay.
I bowed like a reed at your touch. You disrobed me with your words
and left.

Time passes.

Sweet woodruff nests in my hair.
Fieldfares sleep in my ears.
Blankets of moss veil my eyes.
Foxgloves grow out of my fingers.

Time passes.

I fall,
deeper into darkness, soaking in to the holy dirt, and dream of night. A
black cassocked man moving upon the mills and hushed sloping hills,
ready to give last rites to the day.
I dream of rippled ribbons of light falling on ponds clothed with life,
of wild stoats playing on the soft folds of creation.
I dream of the sweet meadow grass quietly bedded between sleeping lovers'
legs.
I dream of the places and spaces you inhabited under my skin.
I dream of song lines. Of the soles of your feet and how they tread
upon my being.
With each step you could sing me back into existence...

I dream of silence.

Of twisting and turning in my sadness, of falling
and finally finding the ground of my being.
I dream of birth.
Death-less wooded tendrils, climbing out and up and through,
touched by sky and bathed in light.
I dream of my again-making.
Of cradling life as it nestles itself into the curve of my boughs.
I dream of being loved.
I dream.

november

oaks are dancing now
as free as spring daffodils
the fall of a leaf

winter

billions of flakes
falling softly through the night
an act of mercy

She is...

A crooked wind-shaped tree.
Entangled roots that reach out
to touch the pain in you
she can see.
She's the bird you swallowed
that lives in your heart,
so tender & loving it tore you apart.
She's the wings that you grew
which took you & flew
to places you dreamed to see.
She is bloodied & broken,
a home of unspoken stones
that stick in your shoe.
She is bed-socks & dominoes,
quiet nights & monotones.
The eddying of sleep
And thoughts that creep
over mountain & moor & glen.
An astronomical collision,
star-fall & stardust, dark & night.
The first incision, the last excision.
Prayer, pain & fright.
She is hope stretched wide like your arms,
dreams spread like a bedsheet.
She is feeble & strong
and loud with song, she delights
in the earth as she moves.
Moves through you like rain,
no shame, no shame.
That she moves like clouds
through rain.
She is necessary.
She is you. She is life.
She is a knife that can cut you from boredom.
She is a knife that can cut you.

www.ingramcontent.com/pod-product-compliance
Ingram Content Group UK Ltd.
Pitfield, Milton Keynes, MK11 3LW, UK
UKHW041934030225
454602UK00004B/329

9 781916 830271